THE POWERS

OF THE

FEDERAL GOVERNMENT

OVER

SLAVERY!

BY ANDREW J. WILCOX.

BALTIMORE:
1862.

THE POWERS

OF THE

GOVERNMENT.

In a former publication, a Remedy for the Defects of the Constitution, I endeavored to show what power the Government had over the subject of slavery, as granted to it by the people, in the particular clauses of the Constitution, bearing on that subject.

Since then, the President has issued his proclamation; the first four and last paragraphs of which is in the words following:

"I, Abraham Lincoln, President of the United States of America, and Commander-in-Chief of the Army and Navy thereof, do hereby proclaim, that hereafter, as heretofore, the war will be prosecuted for the object of practically restoring the Constitutional relations between us and the people thereof, in which States that relation is or may be suspended or disturbed."

"That it is my purpose, upon the next meeting of Congress, to again recommend the adoption of a practical measure, tendering pecuniary aid to the free acceptance or rejection of all the Slave States, so called, the people whereof may not be in rebellion against the United States, and which States may then be in rebellion against the United States, and which States may then have voluntarily adopted, or thereafter may voluntarily adopt, immediate or gradual abolishment of slavery within their respective Cities, and that the efforts to colonize persons of African descent, with their consent, upon this Continent or elswhere, with the previously obtained consent of the Governments existing then will be continued."

"That on the first day of January in the year of our Lord one thousand eight hundred and sixty-three, all persons held as slaves within any State or designated part of a State, the people whereof shall then be in rebellion against the United States, shall be thenceforward and forever free; and that the Executive Government of the United States, including the military and naval authority thereof, will recogonize and maintain the freedom of such persons, and will do no act or acts to repress such persons, or any of them, in any efforts that they may make for their actual freedom."

That the Executive will, on the 1st day of January aforesaid, by proclamation, designate the States and parts of States, if any, in which the people thereof respectively shall then be in rebellion against the United States; and the fact that any State or people thereof shall, on that day, be in good faith represented in the Congress of the United States, by members chosen thereto at elections wherein a majority of the qualified voters of such States shall have participated, shall, in the absence of strong counteracting testimony, be deemed conclusive evidence that such State, and the people thereof, are not in rebellion against the United States; that attention is hereby called to an act of Congress, entitled "An Act to make an additional Article of War," approved March 13th, 1862, &c.

Then follows a paragraph containing the Article of War providing for the non-return of fugitive slaves, those sections of the Confiscation Act which hold out inducements for negroes to become fugitives from their masters, and another, saying that the "Executive will, in due time, recommend that all citizens of the United States, who shall have remained loyal thereto throughout the rebellion, shall, upon the restoration of the constitutional authority between the United States and their respective States and people—if the relations shall have been suspended or disturbed, be compensated for all losses by acts of the United States, including the loss of slaves."

I shall take it for granted, that our Constitution was made for all contingencies, at least for a contingency like the present. In the preamble it is said, that the Constitution was "ordained and established to form a more perfect Union, ***establish justice, insure*** *domestic tranquility, provide for the common defence, promote the general welfare,"* &c.

This language is either false, or the idea that the Constitution was not intended to meet a case like the present, and that the *lex necessitate* must govern is false.

Although the President does not say by virtue of what authority he issues this proclamation, and although he does not even say that it was done by virtue of any authority, yet, I presume, it was intended to have been issued constitutionally, and under the 1st clause of the 8th section of the 1st article, in these words; "To lay and collect taxes, duties, imposts and excises; to pay the debts and *provide for the common defence and general welfare of the United States;* but all duties, imposts and excises shall be uniform throughout the United States."

This power was granted by the people to the Congress, and not the President of the United States. The precise words used are "that the Congress shall have power to lay and collect taxes," &c. The first question that would arise is: Can Congress delegate powers granted to it by the people to another branch of the government? On this question I do not think there can possibly be any difference of opinion, but will suppose that it could, then then the question would arise: Has it done so? This must be answered in the negative. But I will again make the supposition, that Congress will legalize the acts of the President, then the question would arise: Has Congress the power, under this clause, to emancipate slaves?

On this point, Patrick Henry, in the Virginia Convention, said that "With respect to that part of the proposal, which says that every power not granted remains with the people, it must be *previous* to adoption or it will involve this country in inevitable destruction. To talk of it as a thing subsequent; not as one of your inalienable rights; is leaving it to the casual opinion of the Congress who shall take up the consideration of that matter. They *will not reason* with you about the effect of this Constitution. They will not take the opinion of this committee concerning its operation. They will construe it as as they please. If you place it subsequently, let me ask the consequences. Among *ten thousand implied* powers which *they may assume*, they *may*, if we be engaged in war, *liberate* every one of your slaves if they please, and this must and will be done by men, a majority of whom have not a common interest with you."

"They will therefore have no feeling for your interests. It has been repeatedly said here, that the great object of national Government was national defence. *That power which is intended for security and safety, may be rendered detestable and oppressive.* If they give powers to the General Goveroment to provide for the general defence, the means must be commensurate to the end. All the means in the possession of the people must be given to the Government, which is entrusted with the public defence. In this State there are 236,000 blacks and there are many in several other States. But there are few or none in the Northern States, and yet if the Northern States shall be of opinion that our number are numberless. They may call forth every national resource."

"*May Congress not say that every black man must fight.* Did we see a little of this last war? we were not so hard pushed as to make emancipation general. But acts of assembly passed that every slave who would go to the army should be free, another thing will contribute to bring this event about. Slavery is detested. We feel its fatal effects. *We deplore* it with all the pity of humanity. Let all these considerations at some future period press with full force on the minds of Congress. Let that urbanity, which I trust will distinguish America, and the necessity of national defence; let all these things operate on their minds they *will search* that paper and see *if they have power of manumission.* And have they not Sir? have they not power to provide for the general defence and welfare? *May they not think that these call for the abolition of slavery? May they not pronounce all slaves free*, and will they not be warranted by that power? There is no ambigous implication or logical deduction. The paper speaks to the point. They have the power in clear unequivocal terms and will clearly and certainly exercise it. *As much as I deplore slavery, I see that prudence forbids its abolition. I deny* that the general Government *ought to set them free*, because a decided majority of the States have not the ties of sympathy and fellow feeling for those whose interests would be affected by their emancipation. The majority of Congress is to the north, and the slaves are to the south."

"In this situation, I see a great deal of the property of the people of Virginia in jeopardy, and their peace and tranquility gone. I repeat it again that *it would rejoice my very soul that every one of my fellow beings was emancipated.* As we ought with gratitude to admire that decree of heaven, which has remembered us among the free, we ought to lament and deplore the necessity of holding our fellow men in bondage. *But is it practicable by any human means to liberate them without producing the most dreadful and ruinous consequences?* We ought to possess them in the manner we inherited them from our ancestors, *as their manumission is incompatable with the felicity of our Country.* But we ought to soften, as much as possible the rigor of their unhappy fate. I know that in a variety of particular instances, the legislature, listening to complaints, have admitted their emancipation. Let me not dwell on this subject. I will only add that this as well as every other property of the people of Viginia, is in jeopardy and put in the hands of those who have no similarity of situation with us. This is a *local* matter and I can see no propriety in subjecting it to Congress."

"With respect to subsequent amendments proposed by the worthy member I am distressed when I hear the expression. It is a new one altogether, and such a one as stands against every idea of fortitude and manliness in the States, or any one else. Evils admitted in order to be removed subsequently, and *tyranny submitted to* in order to be excluded by subsequent alteration are things totally new to me."

Elliot's Debates on Fed. Constitution, page 533.

It will be remembered, that Patrick Henry was one of the most violent of the opponents of the Constitution; and on this occasion, being his last speech before the question was put to the House, used all the rhetorical and logical powers of which he was capable, in making the strongest possible case against the Constitution, so that he may be considered as a prejudiced witness.

The principal question in *all* the conventions was on the division of powers, between the State and Federal government. The friends of the Constitution claiming, as we shall hereafter see, that (even without the amendments which have since been made, particularly the 9th and 10th here referred to) the government was one of limited powers; that only such powers as were enumerated were intended to be granted, and that these powers could not be enlarged upon. Whilst the opponents of the Constitution, among the most formidable of whom was Patrick Henry, denied this position, and said, that the Constitution, especially this and the 18th clause of this section and article, granted to the government unlimited powers, and would effect a consolidation of the States. Patrick Henry, in this speech says, that if that part of the system, "which says that every power not granted remains with the people," would be inserted, previous to the adoption of the Constitution, it would then be satisfactory even to those who agreed with him, and that the general government would not be able to assume any implied powers, which they would do, (even if the Constitution did not warrant the assumption) as it then was, and Congress could not then imply any power, under the power of providing for the general defence in time of war, to emancipate slaves. It was not the *time when* the amendments should be made, that would prevent the general government from using this unlimited power, but it was the amendments themselves. Although this very amendment had been proposed by nearly all the conventions of which we have the proceedings, and which sat prior to Virginia, yet it was repeatedly said, in the Convention of that State, that these amendments never would be made. Another point here made was that although Patrick Henry deplored slavery, and that it would rejoice his very soul to see all slaves emancipated, yet he thought it was not practicable by any human means to liberate them without producing the most dreadful and ruinous consequences, would be altogether incompatable with felicity of the country, and being a *local* matter, in subjecting it to Congress under the Constitution, as it then was, would be submitting to tyranny in order to afterwards exclude it by subsequent alteration.

Gov. Edmund Randolph, also a member of the Virginia Convention, in reply to Patrick Henry said, that. "That honorable gentlemen and some others have *insisted* that the abolition of slavery will result from it, and at the same time have complained that it encourages its continuation.

The inconsistency proves, in some degree, the *futility* of their arguments. But if it be not *conclusive, to satisfy* the committee, that there is no danger of enfranchisement taking place, I beg leave to refer them to the *paper itself.* I hope that there is none here who, considering the subject in the calm light of philosophy, will advance an objection dishonorable to Virginia; that at the moment they are securing the rights of their citizens, an objection is started that there is a spark of hope that those unfortunate men, now held in bondage, may, by the operation of the General Government, be made *free. But if any gentleman be terrified by this agprehension let him read the system. I ask and I will ask again and again till I be answered,* (*not by declamation*) *where is the part that has a tendency to the abolition of slavery? Is it* the clause which says that "the migration or importation of such persons as any of the States now existing shall think proper to admit, shall not be prohibited by Congress prior to the year 1808." This is an exception from the power of regulating commerce, and the restriction is only to continue till 1808. Then Congress can, by the exercise of that power, prevent future importations; but does it *affeet the existing* state of slavery? *Were it right here to mention what passed in convention on the occasion, I might tell you that the Southern States, even South Carolina herself, conceived this property to be secure by these words. I believe whatever we may think here that there was not a member of the Virginia delegation who had the smallest suspicion of the abolition of slavery. Go to their meaning. Point out the clause where this formidable power of emancipation is inserted.*"

"But another clause of the Constitution proves the *absurdity* of the supposition. The words of the clause are, "no person held to service or labor in one State, under the laws thereof, escaping into another, shall in consequence of any law or regulation therein, be discharged from such service or labor, but shall be delivered up on claim of the party to whom such service or labor may be due." *Every one knows that slaves are held to service and labor.* And when authority is given to owners of slaves to vindicate their property, *can* it be supposed they can be deprived of it? If a citizen of this State, in consequence of this clause, can take his runaway slave in Maryland can it be seriously thought that after taking him and bringing him home he could be made free?"

"I observed that the honorable gentleman's proposition came in a truly *questionable* shape, and is still *more extraordinary* and *unaccountable* for another consideration. That although we went article by article through the Constitution, and although we did not expect a general review on the subject, (as a most comprehensive view had been taken of it before it was regularly debated,) yet we are carried back to the clause giving that *dreadful*(?)power for the general welfare. *Pardon me if I remind you of the true state of that business.* I appeal to the candor of the honorable gentlemen, and if he thinks it an improper appeal, I ask the gentleman here *whether* there be a *general indefinite* power of providing for the general welfare? *The power is* to lay and collect taxes, duties, imposts and excises; to pay the debts and provide for the common defence and general welfare. "So that they can only raise money by these means in order to provide for the common defence and general welfare. No man who reads it, can say it is general, as the honorable gentleman represents it. You must *violate every rule of construction and common sense if you sever it from the power of raising money and annex it to any thing else in order to make it that formidable power which it is represented to be.*"—(Ibid, 3rd vol., page 541.)

Gov. Randolph was not only a member of the Federal Convention, in which the Constitution was adopted, but it was on the basis of his resolutions principally framed. If it can be supposed that any one understood what it was intended that the Constitution should mean, it certainly was he. He does unequivocally say, in this speech, that not only he, but every member in the Convention from the Southern States, fully understood what the intention of those were who framed the Constitution, in regard to the subject of slavery. His words are that "were it right here to tell what passed in Convention, (Federal) on the occasion, *I might tell you that the Southern States, even South Carolina herself, conceived this property to be secure by these words.*" Again, "I believe, *whatever* we may think *here*, that there was not a member of the Virginia delegatiou who had *the smallest suspicion of the abolition of slavery.*" The italics here are his own. This seems to favor the idea that this clause in respect to the "migration or importation of such persons as any of the states then existing should think proper," was regarded as a sacred compromise, on which the slavery question should forever rest. But irrespective of all compromises and private understandings, he goes to the law as laid down in the Constituti n, and asks Patrick Henry and his friends to "point out the clause where this formidable power of emancipation is inserted." "Where is the part that has a tendency to the abolition of slavery? He does not wish to be answered by declamation either. A *conclusive answer* that *no* such power resides in the government, was the clause before quoted in respect to the migration or importation of slaves. But if that is not sufficient to prove the absurdity of the supposition, he quotes the clause, "that no person held to service or labor in one State, under the laws thereof, escaping into another, shall in consequence of any law or regulation therein, be discharged from such service.or labor, but shall be delivered up on claim of the party to whom such service may be due." For fear that it may be misinterpreted, as is now frequeutly done, he declares that every one knows that the terms held to service or labor was intended to mean slaves. Again, least his silence on the clause which provides for the general welfare should be taken as an admission of Patrick Henry's declaration, whom he accuses of endeavoring to get a snap judgment against him, he states what the convention understood was the meaning of the clause. He says, "pardon me if I remind yon of the true state of that business. I appeal to the candor of the honorable gentleman, and if he thinks it an improper appeal, I ask the gentleman here, whether there be a general indefinite power of providing for the general welfare?"

The power is, "to lay and collect taxes, duties, imposts and excises to pay the debts and provide for the common defence and general welfare." Why should the provision to provide for the common defence and general welfare be connected with that to raise taxes, &c? The opponents to the Constitution on all occasions declared that if this Constitution was adopted that all debts of the United States, both foreign and domestic, which had accumulated under the articles of confederation, would be repudiated, which would bring on another foreign war. This clause gives the power to raise the money to pay the debts, which, if not satisfactory to foreign nations and they will war with us, we will provide for the general welfare by applying this money for self defence. "So that they can only raise money by these means." To sever it (the power to providc for the common defence and general welfare) from the power of raising money, and annex it to anything else, especially to the power to abolish slavery, in order that, the war power would become the more formidable, as Patrick Henry represented, it would be, "every rule of construction and common sense must be violated." Ex-President Madison, also a member of both Federal and State conventions, on the same occasion, used the following words, in reply to Patrick Henry, he said: "I was struck with surprise when I heard him express himself alarmed with respect to the emancipation of slaves. Let me ask if they should even attempt it, if it will not be an ursupation of power? There is no power to warrant it in that paper. If there be I know it not. But why should it be done? says the honorable gentleman for the general welfare, it will infuse strength in our system. Can any member of this committee suppose that it will increase our strength? Can any one believe that the American councils will come into a measure which will strip them of there property, discourage and alienate the affections of five thirteenths of the Union. Why was nothing of this sort arrived at before, I believe such an idea never entered into any American breasts, nor do I believe it ever will enter into the heads of those gentlemen who substitute unsupported suspicions for reasons." Ibid page 561.

President Madison was of the opinion that even an attempt to emancipate slaves, under the war power, would be an usurpation of power on the part of the Government. His opinion is also valuable in respect to the allegation that emancipation will infuse strength into our system. The idea is so nonsensical, as to cause him to put the interrogative, "Can any member of this committee suppose that it will increase our strength? The same question might now be asked and could be practically more answered, that instead of its being a means of strength to the Government, in the present contest, it has surely been a means of weakness. It has divided the loyal and united the disloyal. It has thrown upon the Government, for support, many thousands of contrabands who, it is said, do not earn even their support under masters.

On another occasion, when the Cod fishery bill was before the House of Represenatives, in the session of 1790, Jas. Madison, on this particular clause and the general theory of our Constitution said: "I, sir, have always conceived, I believe, those who proposed the Constitution conceived, it is still more fully known and more material to observe, that those who ratified the Constitution conceived, that this is not an indefinite government, deriving its powers from the general terms prefixed to the specified powers; but a limited government, tied down to the specified powers which explain and define the general terms.

It is to be recollected, that the terms "common defence and general welfare," as here used, are not novel terms, first introduced into this Constitution. They are terms familiar in their construction and well known to the people of America. They are repeatedly found in the old Articles of Confederation, where, although they are susceptible of as great a latitude as can be given them by the context here, it was never supposed or pretended that they conveyed any such powers, as is now assigned to them. On the contrary it was always considered clear and certain that the old Congress was limited to the enumerated powers, and that the enumeration limited and explained the general terms. I ask the gentlemen themselves, whether it it was ever supposed or suspected that the old Congress could give away the money of the States to bounties to encourage agriculture, or for any other purpose they pleased? If such a power had been possessed by any body it would have been much less important, or have borne a very different character from that universally ascribed to it.''

"The novel idea now annexed to those terms, and never before entertained by the friends or enemies of the government, will have a further consequence which cannot have been taken into the view of the gentleman.''

"There are consequences, Sir, still more extensive which, as they follow clearly from the doctrine combatted, must either be admitted or the doctrine must be given up. If Congress can employ money indefinitely to the general welfare, and are the sole and supreme judges of the general welfare, they may take the care of religion into their own hands; they may appoint teachers in every State, county and parish, and pay them out of the public treasury; they may take into their own hands the education of children, establishing in like manner schools throughout the Union; they may assnme the provision for the poor; they may undertake the regnlation of all roads, other than post roads; in short every thing from the highest object of state legislation down to the most minute object of police, would be thrown under the power of Congress: for every object I have mentioned would admit of the application of money and might be called, if Congress pleased, provisions for the general welfare.''

In short, Sir, without going farther into the subject, which I should not have touched at all but for the reasons already mentioned, I venture to declare it as my opinion, that were the power of Congress to be established in the latitude contended for, it would subvert the very foundation and transmute the very nature of the limited government, established by the people of America; and what inferences might be drawn or what consequences ensue from snch a step, it is incumbent on us all to consider.''

Mr. Williamson, on the same occasion said, that, "the common defense and general welfare, in the hands of a good politician, may supersede every part of our Constitution and leave us in the hands of time and chance."—Ibid, 4th vol., pages 436-7-8.

Mr. Wilson, in the Pennsylvania Convention, said, on the theory of our government that; "A proposition to adopt a measure that would have supposed that we were throwing into the general government every power, not expressly reserved by the people, would have been spurned at in that house, with the greatest indignation, even in a single government, if the powers of the people rest on the same establishment as is expressed in this Constitution, a bill of rights is by no means a necessary measure."

"But in a government, consisting of enumerated powers, such as is proposed for the United States, a bill of rights would not only be unnecessary, but, in my humble jndgment, highly imprudent. In all societies there are many powers and rights which cannot be particularly enumerated. A bill of rights annexed to a constitution, is an enumeration of the powers reserved. If we attempt an enumeration, every thing that is not enumerated is presumed to be given. The consequence is, that an imperfect enumeration would throw all implied power into the scale of government, and the rights of the people would be rendered incomplete. On the other hand, an imperfect enumeration of the powers of government, reserves all implied power to the people, and by that means the Constitution becomes incomplete, but of the two, it is much safer to run the risk on the side of the Constitution, for an omission in the enumeration of the power of government is neither so dangerous nor important, as an omission in the enumeration of the rights of the people." Elliot's Deb., Fed. Con., 2 vol., page 4091.

Mr. McKean, on the same subject, in the Pennsylvania Convention, also said: "Again, because it (a bill or declaration of rights) is unnecessary, for the powers of Congress, being derived from the people, in the mode pointed out by this constitution, and being therein enumerated and positively granted, can be no other than what this positive grant conveys." (Locke, on civil government, vol. 2, B 2, chap. 2, sect. 140, and in the 13th chap. sec 152.)

"With respect to executive officers, they have no manner of authority, auy of them, beyond what is by positive grant and commission delegated to them"—Ibid, page 498.

This opinion, supported by the authority of an eminent writer on civil government, is conclusive in respect to executive officers, "the chiefest among whom" is the President of the United States.

Alexander Hamilton, in the New York Convention, on this same subject, said, that "The powers of the new government are general, and calculated to embrace the aggregate interests of the Union, and the general interest ot each State, so far as it stands in relation to the whole. The object of the State governments is to provide for their internal interests, as unconnected with the United States, and as composed of minute parts or districts." (Ibid page 259.)

"Again it has been asserted, that the interests, habits and manners of the thirteen States are different, and hence it is inferred, that no general free government can suit them. This diversity of habits, &c., has been a favorite theme with those who are disposed for a division of our empire, and like many popular objections, seems to be founded on fallacy. I acknowledge, that the local interests of the States are in some degree various, and that there is some difference in the manners and habits. But this, I will presume to affirm, that from New Hampshire to Georgia, the people of America are as uniform in their interests and manners as those of any established in Europe. This diversity to the eye of the speculatist, may afford some marks of characteristic discrimination, but can not form an impediment to the regular operation of those general powers which the Constitution gives to the United Government. Where the laws of the Union to new model the internal police of any State; were they to alter or abrogate, at a blow, the whole of its criminal and civil institutions; were they to penetrate the recesses of domestic life, and control in all respects the private conduct of individuals, there might be more force in the objection, and the same Constitution which was happily calculated for one State, might sacrifice the welfare of another. Though the difference of interests may create some difficulty and apparent partiality in the first operations of government, yet the same spirit of accommodation, which produced the plan under discussion, would be exercised in lessening the weight of unequal burthens, add to this, that under the regular and gentle influence of general laws, these varying interests will be constantly assimilating, till they embrace each other and assume the same complexion." (Ibid page 261, &c.)

This speech was in answer to Gov. Clinton, who objected to the Union and Constitution, on the ground that there would not be sufficient safety in the general government. That by small and gradual encroachments, which would not inspire a general spirit of resistance, designs unfavorable to the institutions, of the States could not be frustrated and punished. That the interests of the States was so dissimilar, that the laws made in pursuance of the Constitution would operate most disadvantageously and cruelly upon all the States. The only great dissimilarity existing in the interests of the States, was in regard to slavery, to which Alexander Hamilton replies; "Were the laws of the Union to new model the internal police of any State; were they to alter or abrogate at a blow the whole of its civil and criminal institutions, there might be more force in the objections, and the same Constitution which was happily calculated for one State, might sacrifice the welfare of another." How far this may apply to the present time, let others determine.

On the 18th clause of the 8th section of the 1st article, (To wit: "To make all laws which shall be necessary and proper for carrying into execution the foregoing powers, and all other powers vested by this Constitution in the Government of the United States, or in any department or officer thereof,") denominated the sweeping clause, and which must furnish all necessary power for carrying into execution the powers of the Constitution, Gov. Randolph, ou another occasion, said, that "the sweeping clause, as it is called, is much dreaded. I find that I differ from several gentlemen on this point. This formidable clause does not in the least increase the powers of Congress. It is only inserted for greater caution and to prevent the possibility of encroaching upon the powers of Congress. No sophistry will be permitted to be issued to explain away any of those powers, nor can they possibly assume any other power but what is contained in the Constitution, without absolute usurpation. Another security is, that if they attempt such an usurpation the influence of the State Governments will nip it in the bud of hope. I know this government will be cautiously watched. The smallest assumption of power wili be sounded in alarm to the people and followed by bold and active opposition. I hope that my countrymen will keep guard against every arrogation of power. I shall take notice of what the honorable gentlemen said with respect to the power to provide for the general welfare. The meaning of this clause has been perverted to alarm our apprehensions. The whole clause has not been read together. It enables Congress "to lay and collect taxes, duties, imposts and excises; to pay the debts and provide for the common defence and general welfare of the United States; but all duties, imposts, and excises shall be uniform throughout the United States." The plain and obvious meaning of this is, that no more duties, taxes, imposts and excises shall be laid than are sufficient to pay the debts and provide for the common defence and general welfare of the United States." (Elliott's debates 3rd vol. page 209, &c.) Here we have, in the plainest language, and the briefest space possible, the opinion of one who may be called the founder of our Constitution, on those important parts of the Constitution which confer all power to the Government.

William R. Davie, in the North Carolina Convention, on the subject of powers granted to the Federal Government, said "Mr. Chairman, permit me, Sir, to make a few observations on the operation of the clause so often mentioned. This Constitution, as to the powers therein granted, is constantly to be the supreme law of the land. Every power ceded by it must be executed without being counteracted by the laws or constitutions of the individual States. Gentlemen should distinguish, that it is not the supreme law, in the exercise of a power not granted. It can be supreme only in cases consistent with the powers specially granted, and not usurpations. (Ibid 4th Vol., page 187.)

Chas. Pinckney, in the South Carolina Convention said: "The

distinction which has been taken, between the nature of the Federal and State Government appeared to be conclusive that in the former no powers could be executed or assumed, but such as were expressly delegated ; that in the latter the indefinite power was given to the government, except on points that were by express compact reserved to the people."

Charles Cotesworth Pinckney, in the same Convention, on the question of slavery as settled by the Constitution, said : that "By this settlement, we have secured an unlimited importation for twenty years, nor is it declared that the importation shall then be stopped. It may be continued, we have a security that the general government can never emancipate them, for no such authority is granted, and it is admitted on all hands, that the general government has no powers but what are expressly granted by the Constitution, and that all rights not expressed were reserved by the several States. We have obtained a right to recover our slaves in any part of America they may take refuge, which is a right we had not before. In short considering all circumstances, we have made the best terms for the security of this species of property it was in our power to make, we would have made better if we could, but on the whole, I do not think them bad."—(Ibid page 277.)

If the President shall yet believe (as he did when writing his inaugural) in that fundamental law maxim, "that the intention of the lawgiver is the law" he will certainly believe, that he can, under no necessity, derive any power from the Constitution to issue his proclamation, on the 1st of January A. D. 1863, emancipating slaves; or he must believe that the statesmen, (herein quoted; all, with one exception, leading members of both Federal and State Conventions, which adopted the Constitution, and who may truly be termed the fathers of our Constitution,) were speaking of that which they did not know.

In order that I may not appear to condemn that policy which I cannot propose a remedy for, I shall here insert my letter of July 21st, to His Excellency the President, which general orders (in reference to employing the negroes as laborers, promulgated a few days afterward) will show, was at that time approved of by him.

Baltimore, July 21st, 1862.

Mr. President:—

I but avail myself of the privilege of an American Citizen, when I address you concerning the conduct of the war. This war in the first place has been caused by the agitation of the slavery question, in the National Councils, by men of extreme views. In the second place, we never shall have a permanent peace until the cause is destroyed. A party evidently largely in the minority, argue that slavery is the cause of the agitation of the slavery question, and therefore the primary cause of the war, with equal force, it may be said that the existence of the negroes is the cause of slavery, and so on, until the cause would be attributed to the Creator himself. We are not now to deal with abstractions. This war is found to be too much of a sad reality. But it is not true that slavery is the cause of the slavery agitation, it has existed in the nation since its formation. Many States have both abolished and established it, by State action, without even causing much agitation within their own borders. It has only been since politicians and demagogues have discovereed the suitablenesss of the subject, for the purpose of manufacturing political capital, (it being about twenty odd years) that this agitation has assumed so great proportions and become so acrimonius. It is evident that the that the Nation would meet with as much success if it should attempt to destroy the Creator himself, and would cause about as much distress, if it should attempt to destroy the negroes, (to either of which causes the war could be abstractly attributed,) as it would if it should attempt to destroy the agitation of the slavery question, by destroying, or in other words, abolishing slavery itself. Without fear of contradiction, I think it can be safely said, that all past legislation, with a view to that end, instead of decreasing has increased this agitation, at a cost almost of the life of the Nation. Nor, do I want to be understood to say, that to get rid of this agitation slavery should be established everywhere. The attempt to establish slavery, anywhere, by National legislation, would be frought with as much agitation as the attempt to abolish it in certain places has already been; but I do want to be understood to say, and I do say, that the only true policy to be pursued by the Nation is to have nothing at all to do with the matter. The opposite policy has been tried, in accordance with the views of each of the extremes, and found wanting. If for nothing more than an experiment, it would now be well to let this matter alone. Besides, being the only true policy, and the only one on which all loyal men can be united under, it is of itself destroying the cause of the war and is moreover the only legal and constitutional course that can be pursued. By virtue of what clause in the Constitution, or what law in accordance therewith, has the administration now power to do anything farther with the matter?

The only clauses on which there possibly could have been any difference of opinion have been fully settled by Congressional action.

The subject of slavery presents, legislatively, three different phases: First in relation to places where it is claimed that Congress has exclusive jurisdiction, for all purposes. Secondly, in relation to places where it is claimed that Congress has a supervisory, amounting pratically to an exclusive jurisdiction; and Thirdly, in relation to places where it is claimed that Congress has concurrent jurisdiction, with the State legislatures. In places of the first and second class the last congress were of the opinion that they had power to legislate on the subject of slavery, which they carried into practice, by abolishing it in those places; whether this was in accordance with the Constitution it would be (now that it is done) to no purpose to argue, and does not very materially effect the question, in so far as it is connected with the war; but in places of the third class, which is of the greatest importance, the preceeding Congress were of the opinion (which they formally embodied into an amendment to the Constitution) that they had no power at all to interfere. This embraces, with the exception of the fugitive slave law and clause, all the power it is claimed the national government has over the matter, and was enacted chiefly by men of radical views. It is now the right of the opposition to demand that they (the radicals) (having exhausted, in their own manner, all the power they themselves claim over this matter) should let the agitation of it alone. This gets rid of the matter as a state institution. But in regard to each individual negro, the question arises what is to be done with the fugltive slave law, in reference to the contrabands. Even in this respect, the above policy could be practically carried out. The Government cannot question the tenure by which these persons are held to service or labor, but until their be a claim made for their services, they (the contrabands) must be regarded as free persons and should be used as such, but (waving all questions of right) let me ask, does policy dictate that they should be employed as laborers in preference to white men, or on an equality with white men in the ranks, which is not elevatiug the negro but degrading our own class, thereby causing dissatisfaction in the army, or should the families of negroes be mantained and supported whilst the families of patriotic volunteers are suffering. I am satisficd that you will not say such is good policy.

Again, the fugitive slave law should and can only be executed through civil officers. If some States have, by their own course, destroyed these officers, they alone should be made to reap the benefit. The military have not been called out to execute the laws, but to put down those who are endeavoring to prevent their execution; much less is it to prevent themselves the execution of the laws, as is supposed by some. Whilst this policy would not assist negroes in running away, it would not at the same time make the men of the army negro catchers. The army can no more accomplish two things, at one and the same time, than an individual. If it is to engage in the African slave trade, the war will necessarily have to take care of itself; but if, by hard and strong blows, it is intended to use it for the purpose of putting an end to the rebellion, abolition and slavery must take care of themselves. Let it once be proclaimed that the army is to have nothing at all to do with the negro question, and there would be no difficulty in filling up the ranks, and all would yet be well. I have the honor to be, Mr. President,

Your most humble
and obedient servant,
ANDREW J. WILCOX.

To His Excellency, Abraham Lincoln.

One word here in regard to the war. If, it (the war) shall be made the means of putting an end to the agitation of the slavery question, which is the only means that will secure the National peace and happiness, not only of the present generation, but of generations yet unborn, then it shall have been to some purpose. If not, then the loss of thousands of lives and the expenditure of millions of dollars will all have been in vain.

www.ingramcontent.com/pod-product-compliance
Lightning Source LLC
LaVergne TN
LVHW011145110826
845150LV00008B/2518

* 9 7 8 1 4 1 8 1 9 1 8 2 5 *